DUMMIES GUIDE TO STARTING YOUR OWN BUSINESS

A Quick Guide to a Successful Entrepreneurship

Robert J. McKeen

TABLE OF CONTENT

INTRODUCTION

According to business owners, starting and growing a business is one of the satisfying ways to make a living though it often comes with some difficulties. Being a successful entrepreneur requires a lot of work and dedication, but it also typically relies on a set of character traits and business practices that successful entrepreneurs share. These characteristics affect every decision an entrepreneur takes and influence both the core values and day-to-day operations of an organization. Are you planning to start a business or you are looking for a way to improve the one you have started already? Either way, by following the instructions and guidance given in this book, you can improve your prospects of beginning a lucrative business or of getting your present one back on track.

It is not always easy to own a business, but if you have the right mindset and develop the right strategy, you can set it up for success. Examine your requirements, create a solid business plan, and file your legal paperwork before opening your business or firm. Once you have an effective business strategy and the financial resources required to achieve your goals, you'll be definitely on your way to launching a profitable business.

We will go through exactly what is expected of any business owner who wants to successfully create, manage, and grow his business or firm both offline and online in the various sections of this book.

Chapter One

GENERATING BUSINESS IDEAS

There is a lot of effort involved in starting a business, including developing a business plan, finding investors, obtaining money, and hiring staff. But before doing anything further, you need to first acquire your business idea. No matter how creative or unique a service or product is, it has to be something that customers are willing to pay for. For someone to come up with that great idea, one must think, be imaginative, and do research. Keep the following in mind when you generate business ideas if you're planning to launch your own business.

HOW TO GENERATE AN IDEA

Think about the goods and services that could improve your life. Make a list of your unique skills and areas of weakness. Consider if there is anything on that list that might improve your way of living. Take some time to reflect on your own experiences. If you give them some consideration and effort, you can undoubtedly come up with a number of products or services that would be useful.

Decide if you want to sell a product or a service. A new business idea's base will probably be one of two things: a product or a service. Each requires some thought and creativity. Before focusing on one over the other, weigh each option's advantages and disadvantages.

• Before you invest in the production required to sell a product, it must first be created or improved if your idea is already in the market.

• The requirement to create and manufacture a new product will be replaced by the provision of a service.

• Even though it is expensive to create new products, those that are successful can be quite lucrative.

• However, it will be challenging to grow your business if you are the only one providing a service, so you'll likely need to hire more staff. Whichever strategy you choose, you will need to invest time and resources in marketing and promotion.

Look for a problem in the market segment that you are knowledgeable about. Have you recently bought anything and you fill the quality of that thing needs to be improved? Is there any service you were not satisfied with recently? Sometimes, someone's dissatisfaction with how things were done inspired them to start a business or create something. A great way to come up with business ideas is to be on the lookout for these problems. It's possible that people share your dissatisfaction with anything, which creates a market for you. Perhaps no one in your community provides bike repairs. You've identified a need that, if it goes unmet, you could supply by providing that service.

Adapt a tried-and-true business idea. You might notice a company doing something well instead of a problem with the current industry. Look into it to see whether you can improve it. By taking an idea one step further than the competitors, you can carve out a space for yourself in the market.

• Google is a superb example of how to improve on an already excellent idea.

• At the time Google started, there were a number of competing internet search engines. Google, however, developed a very accurate algorithm that improved search results. Now you can see how successful Google is. There are a lot of other successful companies or business owners who started by improving the product or services of already existing ones. You too can do the same

Think about the future. Successful businesspeople are inventors. They look to the future, forecast what will prosper, and then put their vision into practice rather than adopting antiquated methods or technologies. This can be done by taking into account the logical development of a product line or the expansion of a service that is provided.

You can think about starting a company that focuses on tools that can help remote teachers as distance learning gains popularity. You can develop a notion that will be unique and, possibly, completely change the market by looking at present trends and advancing them.

Perform an initial consumer study. Although market research is normally only performed once you have an idea, you may still do some early study to see what buyers value. This can help you create a notion based on the needs and desires of others.

Find out what people are searching for most frequently by conducting some web research. The most common search keywords will be shown, and having this knowledge may provide you with some inspiration.

• For a more challenging method of finding popular keywords, you may use a service like Bing Ads or Google Adwords. These also study the most common search terms.

Use your abilities in a different field. Another strategy to come up with a new service or product is to make use of the skills you've developed via prior encounters. You can frequently advance another industry by imaginatively using skills you've gained in one. Leo Fender worked as a radio

Repairer, for example. Using his expertise in electronics and amplification, he developed the first electric guitars. When creating your business thoughts, take into account all of your areas of competence. You might have a talent that transforms a different industry.

MAKING A LIST OF ALL YOUR IDEAS

No matter how little or unimportant a thought may seem, it nevertheless might be worthwhile. Make it a habit to keep an "idea notepad" handy so that you can jot down any and all of your thoughts. You ought to carry this with you at all times since you cannot predict when inspiration will strike. You can do this to put all of your ideas in one convenient spot. Make sure to check it out periodically to see if there are any ideas you can add to or develop.

• You might consider inputting those ideas onto a computer or phone depending on your preference and availability although you can always bring a notebook with you.

• In the event your notebook is lost or damaged, you will have a backup.

• You will be able to precisely and clearly catalog your ideas by using digital storage.

Boost your creative thinking. Try not to be too critical of your ideas at this time. When you're doing this brainstorming, you ought not to feel restricted. Rather, give yourself permission to daydream and see what thoughts might emerge. You can utilize a variety of strategies to foster your imagination or inventiveness and develop ideas.

• If you feel unmotivated or inspired, walk for a few hours each week to boost your health and spark your imagination.

• Numerous studies have demonstrated the benefits of walking for brain health, particularly for creativity.

• Bring your journal along when you're going for walks so you can jot down any thoughts.

• If you're looking for ideas, visit a local store, preferably a sizable department store.

• Next, just stroll through the aisles and write a list of the things you see. What services do they provide? Why do they need to be fixed?

• Take into account the things you haven't seen as well since this will enable you to identify any unavailable yet potentially commercial things.

• Interact with others from different professions.

• If you're creating new software, seek advice from more than simply fellow IT experts.

• Experiment with new things and interact with people from different fields, especially those you are not already familiar with. Examine how people use products or services to improve their lives.

You will be inspired to come up with ideas creatively and from fresh angles as a result of this.

Take a brief pause. Even if they are slightly overused, the tales of people getting brilliant ideas in the restroom are true. When you are not trying to think too hard, your brain often comes up with ideas. You can rest your brain by taking a step back. During that time of relaxation, you should make every effort to avoid thinking about your business, your product or service, or anything else related to it. Redirect your focus to a book, a walk, a movie, or whatever other fun activity that interests you. You have no idea when you might suddenly come up with the answer to the problem you've been battling throughout your break.

Get plenty of sleep. Along with breaks, sleep is essential for keeping your brain alert. Make the decision to get a good night's sleep if you want to keep your brain performing at its optimum. Keep your pen and jotter near your bed as well. Sometimes breakthroughs or original concepts appear in dreams.

LOOKING AT YOUR SUGGESTIONS

Compare the benefits and drawbacks of your plan. Even if you have a great concept, you might not have the means to carry it out. Think about the possibility that you could truly execute this plan before moving on. For example, starting a restaurant business might be a very good idea in your list but you also need to consider the chance that you can start and grow it successfully. If you have never worked in a restaurant and have not attended culinary school, it might be quite challenging to fulfill your ambition of owning one.

Check to see if anyone else has thought of this before. There is a strong probability that if you've got an idea, someone else has already had it. Check to see if a business concept of yours has already been put into practice. You don't want to invest time and money developing a concept for months just to discover at the last minute that it has already been used by someone else. To avoid this, be sure to perform a thorough investigation and ascertain if your concept is truly novel.

• Use a web search engine as a starting point. Add the solution or thing you can think of.

• Since it's possible that you won't find the ideal match, look into every possibility to see whether anyone else has already started a business that is comparable to yours.

• This method is far more complicated and time-consuming than conducting an online search.

• You could possibly need to consult a patent law specialist in order to use this method efficiently.

Investigate the competition. If you find that someone else came up with the same idea before you, don't become irritated. A lot of new businesses have an intense rivalry when they first start up, which they conquer by providing superior products or services. You must now research any potential competitors.

• Begin trading with the rivalries. Purchase their product or service to discover for yourself how they operate.

• By closely examining your competitors' operations, you can find strategies to outperform them.

• Interact with the customers of competitors. Formally or informally survey the customers of your competitors.

• Ask them directly about their levels of satisfaction and unhappiness so you may adjust the way you operate to address their problems.

• Examine your competitors' web presence. There may be blogs or review websites that discuss your competitors.

• Carefully examine these to determine if you've discovered any criticisms of the operations of your competitors.

Share your idea with friends, family, and colleagues. Before investigating customers, consult with someone you are confident will tell you the truth. Present to them your idea and describe how it will help the market grow. Sincerely inquire if they would buy your product or service. By doing this, you can get a few trustworthy people to give your idea a preliminary assessment. They will either endorse your idea, provide constructive criticism, or let you understand if they don't think it will work. Irrespective of the type, you must pay attention to every input.

Talk to potential customers. Once you've produced what you feel to be a great idea and informed a few close friends, you ought to branch out and see whether or not there is a customer base for you. You can try a variety of things to see if people will be willing to utilize your business.

• Conduct face-to-face interviews. Visit locations where clients for your business may be. For example, if you're developing a novel fishing lure, talk to employees operating in the fishing section at various sporting goods stores.

• After briefly outlining your prospective business, ask clients if they have any interest in that specific sector of the market.

• Keep conversations short; even while certain individuals may find themselves interested in continuing, many others will probably get annoyed if you occupy too much of their time.

• Emailing participants with questionnaires. It is simple and quick to create tiny surveys using a program like Google Forms.

• Consider sharing the surveys with your personal contacts and asking them to do them as well for their personal networks.

Determine risks and difficulties. Every company plan contains risks, whether they are financial or psychological. There could be many difficulties, including a lack of finance, a conflict with your business partner, or the severing of your personal ties. Prepare for these potential risks. Looking down the road will help you identify any obstacles you might encounter. By thinking about them beforehand, you may improve your chances of managing such threats successfully and maintaining your business. Consider the following suggestions to get past your obstacles since many new firms will experience some difficulties.

• Only partner with dependable individuals. A bad partner or supplier could have a negative impact on your company. To avoid this problem, work with people you feel you can trust.

• Before taking any further action, always verify your funds.

• One of the main causes of startup failure is a lack of funding.

• Hold off on implementing your idea if you lack the cash to avoid debt or bankruptcy.

• Be receptive to change. The market may change even if your business is a success. If you want to stay competitive, you must adjust to these developments.

• Overcome failure. Many new businesses fail. Recognize that this does not necessarily have to be the end and that you can continue with a better strategy and more resources.

Make sure your plan can be implemented. After performing every one of these, you must determine whether or not your plan can be carried out. Your idea is examined taking into account a variety of elements. To decide whether you should adhere to your plan, carefully weigh each one.

• Take into account every survey and interview you've conducted. Your plan has a market, right?

• Be honest with yourself; don't deceive yourself into thinking there would certainly be a demand if few people expressed interest.

• If no one will buy your stuff, try another idea.

• How competitive are you? You'll have to work really hard to beat the competition if it's tough.

• If you want to have a chance, take the time to explain in detail how you will perform better than your competitors.

• Analyze the costs of your plan. Although there is a big market for your idea, you must decide whether it is economically feasible.

• *Is* the launch and ongoing costs disproportionately expensive? You would possibly want to reconsider that too.

• Take into account your finance sources as well.

• Calculate the expenses related to your plan in addition to the anticipated income.

Sort out your ideas. If you have multiple ideas, list them from greatest to worst. After they have responded to all the previous questions, evaluate their performance. Then order them starting with the greatest at the top. As a result, you can be sure that your attempts are focused on your best idea. Ideas towards the bottom of the list ought to either be abandoned or greatly improved before attempting to implement them.

Chapter Two

LAUNCHING A BUSINESS

An excellent company idea is only the beginning of the road to success. For it to succeed, you must take a few steps to launch it successfully. To strengthen your business idea and set yourself up for success, you should consider doing the following:

DEVELOPING A BUSINESS PLAN

Every successful business has a business plan. Your business plan describes the organizational structure of the business, the products or services that it will offer, and the marketing strategies it will employ. A business plan will help you discover any potential issues before you begin operating a business.

- ➢ A Business Plan for Launching
- ➢ Utilize a sample business plan, and focus on your unique selling points.
- ➢ Make it simple and brief
- ➢ For the executive, write a synopsis.
- ➢ Specify your business' mission and business plan.

- ➢ Analyze the conditions in your market.
- ➢ Describe the service or item you are offering.
- ➢ Outline each managerial and operational position.
- ➢ Come up with a marketing and sales strategy.
- ➢ Provide a thorough description of a financial plan, including anticipated costs, funding, and income.
- ➢ Add an appendix containing a synopsis of the materials described above.

Your company can stay on course with a solid business plan, especially while facing obstacles. Nevertheless, let's begin by addressing an important issue before discussing how to write one:

WHAT EXACTLY IS A BUSINESS PLAN?

A business plan is an ongoing document that includes detailed information about the business you run. It describes the items or services your business will provide, the way it will be structured, the market, the advertising strategy you want to apply, the capital required, your cost projections, and the licenses, leasing agreements, as well as other forms of documentation that will be required.

Your business idea's viability must be proven to yourself as well as other people, and that is the main goal of a business plan. The best approach is to take a step back, analyze the idea you have as a whole, and deal with issues that will arise years from now before you start getting into the weeds

Below is a summary of the key elements of a business plan template, along with details on what each one entails. You'll also learn how to draft a business strategy.

• *Use a business plan template*

Before you begin developing your strategy, have a template for a company plan. It simplifies the process and gives you a path to take.

The first step is to create a front page and write a description of the business that lists your products or services and describes how they satisfy a need for your client. The next stage is to concentrate on the executive summary, which includes the goal and vision statements and details of the organizational structure of your business.

The following section of the business plan form will list the market you are targeting or buyer personas. By doing surveys, interviews, and research, you may find out who your potential consumers are, what makes them interested in your product, and what issue it solves for them.

The next step is to give a comprehensive overview of your line of products and services, in addition to details on your pricing policy and the business's competitive edge.

The next stage is to write down your sales and marketing strategies. You'll also specify your growth plan and set objectives and benchmarks for your marketing and sales projects. Then, you'll choose the legal structure your business will operate under (sole proprietorship, partnership, etc.) and any further legal matters that need to be addressed (such as permits, licenses, and health codes). The company will then formulate short- and long-term goals as well as financial projections.

• *Focus on your unique qualities*

Before you begin developing a business strategy, thoroughly consider what makes your business unique. If you're beginning a new ladies' wear business, for example, you'll need to differentiate yourself from the several other athletic gear enterprises that are currently on the market.

What sets yours apart from the competition? Do you aim to design clothing for a specific age group or cultural activity, such as for young girls, women, or elderly women? Do you utilize environmentally friendly materials? Do you give a specific percentage of your earnings to charity? Does your business support having a positive body image?

By being aware of where your brand sits in the market, you can raise brand and product awareness. It is also important to understand that you're not only selling your products or services; you're also selling value and a recognizable brand. Think about and note these critical points before diving into the intricacies of your business plan study.

• *Keep it simple and brief*

Business plans are now more concise and straightforward than ever before. Although it may be tempting to include all of the results of your market research, go into great depth about every single item that you are interested in selling, as well as describe your website in great detail, these things are undoubtedly not helpful in the context of a business plan.

Even if you ought to be conscious of these facts and save them somewhere else, your business plan should only contain the most crucial details. Your business plan should be quick to skim and understand. After discussing this first, very important step in the process, it is now time to begin developing your business plan.

HOW TO WRITE A BUSINESS PLAN

• Write an executive summary

The executive summary is aimed to provide readers with a general understanding of the business's operations and the market before diving into the details.

Pro tip: When you have finished the rest of the plan, it can be helpful to develop an executive summary to make it simpler to highlight the most crucial parts.

The executive summary should be one or two pages long. It should include:

Overview: Briefly describe your business, your location, your goods and services, and your target audience.

Start by describing the organizational structure of the business, the owners' qualifications, and any potential applicants for the first hiring role in the company profile.

Briefly describe the products or services you provide.

The Market: Highlight the major findings from your market study, including how well your product fits into that market.

Financial Considerations: Provide a brief summary of your funding strategies for the business as well as your financial projections.

• **Describe your company's operating model**

After that, you need to establish a business description. Here is where you can put the following information:

✓ A synopsis of your company's operations
✓ A statement of your goal
✓ Information on your position as owner and the structure of the business
✓ Specifics about your location.
✓ A thorough justification of how your products or services actually meet the market demands that your business is aiming to fulfill

• Assess the condition of your market

One of the initial things to think about when testing a business idea is whether there is an audience for it. The level of success your company ultimately achieves will be defined by the market. Who is your ideal client, and why would they want to work with you?

Describe it in detail. If you sell shoes, for example, you can't assume that everyone who goes on the street is one of your potential clients. Your initial target market should be a smaller one, such as teenagers from middle-class families.

What percentage of children in your country are raised in middle-class homes, for example? Might be answered from there.

What kind of footwear is often required?

Is the market growing or staying the same?

Include both a review of earlier studies and your own unique research, whether it was done through interviews, client surveys, or another method. You will also have incorporated an assessment of competition here. In your fictitious situation, you would be answering the following question: What percentage of the market is already held by other shoe companies, and how many are there?

List your strategies for gaining a competitive edge, as well as the benefits and drawbacks of possible competitors.

• Describe your product or service

Here, you can talk about the particulars of what you're providing and how it benefits the clients of your organization. If you are unable to describe how your customers would profit from your business, your idea may not be a good one.

Outline the problem you're attempting to solve in the beginning. After that, describe how you plan to fix the problem and how your product or service fits into the bigger picture. Finally, talk about the competitive landscape: What other companies are providing solutions to this particular problem, and what sets yours apart from theirs?

• Specify each managerial and operational position.

Use this part to describe the unique managerial and organizational structure of the business while keeping in mind the possibility that you can modify it later. Who will be responsible for what? How will each person or group be assigned their roles and duties?

Each team member should have a brief profile that highlights any experience that is pertinent or credentials that can support the case for why they are qualified for the position. It's okay if you are yet to hire people to fill the anticipated jobs; just make sure to indicate the gaps and describe the tasks of those individuals.

- **Make a plan for your sales and marketing**

You may create your comprehensive sales and marketing strategies right here, which will outline how you actually expect to sell your products. Before starting to design your sales and marketing plan, you must have a fully established market study and choose your target buyer personas, or your ideal clients. (You may find guidelines for developing buyer personas here.)

When it comes to the marketing side, you should respond to questions such as:

✓ How exactly do you plan to enter the market?
✓ How do you intend to grow your business?

- ✓ Which routes of distribution would you give top priority?
- ✓ How will you communicate with your customers?
- ✓ You must provide answers to questions like: What is your sales strategy?
- ✓ How will you expand at a larger scale?
- ✓ What will the composition of your sales staff look like going forward? How do you plan to grow it?
- ✓ What is the average price of sale?
- ✓ What number of sales calls will you need to make to seal the deal?

You ought to talk about your pricing strategy when addressing average cost per sale. Give a thorough explanation of a financial plan, including estimated costs, funding, and income. When presenting your financial plan to potential investors, make sure to include your start-up expenses, cost projections, and a fundraising request.

Your start-up cost is the sum of the expected costs of the resources you'll need to start your firm and the actual costs of those resources. Do you rent out an office space? Is it necessary that you have a computer? When you set out these criteria and their accompanying expenditures, you should be truthful and moderate in your estimates. You don't want to run out of money.

You must outline your expenses and then provide exact financial estimations to back them up. This is incredibly important if you're looking for funding for your business. Make sure your financial model is completely correct to provide your business with the best opportunity of obtaining funding from financiers and credit sources.

• Add an appendix containing a summary of the materials described above. As a last step, think about including an appendix to your business strategy. It is not compulsory to include.

Appendix, however, it's a nice place to include any rentals, licenses or authorizations, or other types of legal documentation you want to attach as well as your cover letter, the professional profiles of your teammates, and your co-founders' resumes.

PICK A NAME FOR YOUR COMPANY

The name of your new business is a crucial element. It identifies the name that will be used on official documents as well as in the business plan you will offer to investors. Since your name is going to be determined by the business plan you've developed and what your product delivers, it is better to come up with it after you've created a strategy.

Strategies for Naming a Company. It's easier to make a list and choose your favorite than to name your business. Any names you use except your given name must be registered with your state government in order to inform them that you are doing business under a different name.

Follow these instructions for choosing a name for your business and having it registered with the appropriate authorities to do this.

• Come up with suggestions for names of businesses

The first stage in carefully choosing the best business name is conventional brainstorming. Selecting "[city name] + [service]," such as Atlanta Dentist, can appear to be a simple, straightforward process for some businesses. Due to the fact that it will improve their exposure in local search results, local businesses should think about implementing this.

However, you might want to consider a distinctive brand name if you're beginning a creative business or another type of business that would benefit from a memorable name. In any case, we suggest picking a name that is succinct, memorable, and simple to say and write.

• Look through the trademark database

The next name you choose should be the subject of a trademark search to avoid any costly issues later. The search will inform you if the name you intend to use has been registered or requested by another business. Keep in mind that if you misuse a trademark, the owner may sue you if they have a good reason to.

• **Check to see if your state allows access to the requested name.**

Before registering, make sure the requested name is accessible in your state. Due to the fact that business names are registered on a per-state basis, a company in another state may already be utilizing your name. This should only be a problem if the name is trademarked.

• **Check to see if the domain name is accessible online.**

When choosing a name, you should take into account how it is going to appear as a website domain. That is a straightforward test to determine whether the name is succinct and memorable enough for someone to remember the website's URL.

Once you've chosen the name for your domain, check with domain name registrars to determine whether it's still available. There is nothing worse than coming up with a brilliant business concept and then having to register a domain with a misspelled name, like "businessname-1.com," "business-name.com," or "therealbusinessname.com."

"Businessname.com" is the most readable and memorable alternative, however, none of them are awful choices.

When you find a name you like that is widely available in its original form, register the domain name to make sure no one else does.

- *If you've chosen a distinctive name, register your trademark.*

If you want further security, you can trademark the name of your business. Trademarks give owners the right to use specific words, images, and logos to refer to their goods and services.

- *Include the name of your business (optional).*

You won't likely need to take any further steps after registering your business name. Most of the time, it will happen naturally. There is no need for a different process if you are a newly formed corporation or LLC because your business name will be registered with your state right away.

If you are a sole proprietorship, partnership, corporation, or current LLC and wish to carry on business under a name different than your registered name, you must submit a "Doing Business As" (DBA) name application. You can do this at either your state's government or your county clerk's office, depending on where you are.

If you're not sure what an LLC, corporation, or partnership is, don't worry. These are known as business structures, and they handle your company's top-down management. We talk about how to choose from them later on.

CHOOSING THE RIGHT LEGAL STRUCTURE

The legal system in place for your business may have an impact on your liabilities and tax requirements. The four most common types of business structures are a corporation, a limited liability company, and a sole proprietorship. When forming a firm, you must choose the model that is ideal for you.

How to Choose an Ownership Structure

One of the most crucial legal requirements you must fulfill when beginning a business is selecting an ownership structure, commonly referred to as your business entity or business legal structure. The four types of business structures are listed below:

A SOLE PROPRIETORSHIP (ONE-PERSON BUSINESS)

A sole proprietorship or one-man business is a business whereby there is no legal distinction between the owner and the business; rather, it is owned and run by just one person. It's the simplest way to manage the business. The business you run does not need to have a name other than your own, but if you would prefer it to, you have the option of giving one by registering a "Doing Business As" (DBA) name.

Pros: A sole proprietorship is simple and affordable to set up because the owner has total control over all business decisions. Because the owner of a sole proprietorship is not subject to taxation separately, filing taxes is easier.

Cons: Given that the Business and its Owner are treated as one entity for legal purposes, the owner is individually liable for all of the risks and obligations of the business. Since it has no legal structure that promises repayment if the business fails, it can be considerably more difficult to raise money and find investors or loans.

How Taxes Work

The sole proprietor is responsible for all financial matters, including responsibilities and debts, as well as for managing the business. On a person's personal income tax return, losses and income are taxed at ordinary rates. You also owe payroll taxes, also referred to as self-employment taxes, on your income. The IRS tax forms are shown here.

Use these questions to decide if it's right for you:

- *Will you be the sole employee in the near future?*
- *Are you comfortable shouldering the entire financial burden for the business?*

Choosing this, in that case, would be sensible. If not, think about setting up an LLC or corporation, which would offer you more protection in the case that the company fails.

PARTNERSHIP

A partnership is a single company with two or more owners, each of whom contributes to all aspects of the firm and shares in its profits and losses.

Pros: Forming a business partnership is typically not too complicated. A partnership also doesn't cost too much. When two or more individuals are equally committed to the success of the business and you have access to a variety of people's skill sets and knowledge, you can pool resources.

Cons What if the company fails? Partners would be equally and totally responsible, exactly like a sole proprietor. LLPs, or limited liability partnerships, are a type of partnership that provides defense against this. Partners are accountable for both their own actions and those of their partners. When more than one person is involved in making decisions, there is a possibility of disagreement, so it is crucial to have a formal agreement describing how the expenses and rewards will be allocated.

How Taxes Work

Before you register your business with the state, which is frequently done through the Secretary of State's office, a partnership must first be formed. Separate tax returns for each partner's self-employment are also required. The IRS tax forms are shown here.

Use these questions to decide if it's right for you:

- *Will you be launching the business with someone else, such as a friend or relative?*

If so, choosing this is a wise move for you. A partnership structure is especially helpful if the other investor is a family member to make sure that no one betrays their word.

- *Are you comfortable bearing the company's share of the liability?*

Choosing this, in that case, would be sensible. If not, consider moving to an LLC, corporation, or limited liability partnership, which would provide you with extra security in the event that the business fails.

- *Do you consider yourself skilled at resolving disputes and collaborating with others?*

Working as a team and managing conflicts are essential parts of starting a business with a partner. Instead, if you prefer to operate independently, consider establishing a sole proprietorship.

(LLC) LIMITED LIABILITY COMPANY

Limited liability companies (LLCs) are a type of business structure with a greater complexity compared to partnerships and sole proprietorships but less complex than corporations. They are referred regarded as "pass-through entities" since they do not fall under a different tax regime. Since the majority of states do not place restrictions on LLC ownership, anybody is able to join, including individuals, companies, other LLCs, and even foreign entities. Most states also permit "single-member" LLCs, or businesses with only one owner.

Pros: An LLC's owners have limited liability, which exempts them from being held personally responsible for any financial or legal errors the business may make. The fact that an LLC lowers risk is what makes it such a popular business structure. They are simpler to manage than corporations since there are fewer formalities and regulations to follow.

Cons: Oftentimes more complicated than partnerships or sole proprietorships, LLCs have greater start-up costs. Many venture capital funds are reluctant to invest in LLCs due to the tax repercussions and the aforementioned complexity.

How Taxes Work

Owners, not the LLC, are subject to tax since LLCs benefit from "flow-through" tax treatment. With only one level of assessment, taxes are easier to understand. The IRS tax forms are shown here.

Use these questions to decide if it's right for you:

- *Would you prefer to bear the least degree of accountability for the business's operations and financial outcomes?*

A yes? Then setting up an LLC is a terrific approach to protect your money and property. This is a smart move even if you're starting your own freelance business.

- *Can you afford to pay the LLC fees?*

Even while the costs associated with forming an LLC aren't extremely high, your business will still need to set aside money for them.

CORPORATION

Due to the fact that businesses are considered separate legal entities from their owners, the majority of the rights and responsibilities that apply to individuals also apply to them. Due to its sophistication compared to the other business structures, it is frequently advised for larger, more established enterprises with several employees.

Pros

Only the funds and resources that they have personally contributed are subject to liability; founders, directors, and investors are (usually) not responsible for the company's debts and obligations. They make finding venture capital simple. They provide the best defense for specific assets.

Cons

Compared to other business forms, they have more complicated tax and legal regulations, which can lead to high administrative costs.

How Taxes Work

Corporations are required to pay federal, state, and in certain cases municipal taxes. There are two distinct types of corporations: "C corporations" and "S corporations." C corporations are subject to double taxation. A C corporation must pay taxes on every profit it makes as well as any dividends it distributes to its shareholders.

Dividend payments to shareholders do not qualify as a tax deduction for the corporation. Only the dividends that shareholders pay out to other shareholders are subject to taxation; they are not allowed to deduct any losses that the company suffers.

However, there is just one taxes level that applies to corporations. Here you may find IRS tax forms and find out more about the differences between "C corporations" and "S corporations."

Use these questions to decide if it's right for you:

- Have you secured enough venture capital to turn your little company into a full-fledged corporation?

Although businesses may start off small, they need to have the financial resources to grow. If your business has a list of investors who have made contributions of $1 million or more, it might be time to think about incorporation.

- *Does your organization have an internal accounting team with tax knowledge?*

Corporate tax laws can be complicated, demanding the expertise of accountants with specific understanding. If you already own a team or want to develop one, a corporation may be your best bet.

REGISTERING YOUR BUSINESS

Registering your company comes next after choosing an ownership structure. By using this strategy, you may ensure that you're abiding by the most significant legal constraints.

How to Open an Account for a Business

Once a business concept, company name, and corporate structure are established, it is possible to move on to the even less romantic step of beginning a business—the documentation and legal tasks. Depending on your industry and business structure, this requires signing up with the government, filing taxes, and/or gaining a seller's approval.

• *Select your residence state*

Where are your operations? Choose the state where your company will have its operational base.

Register the name of your business.

Your business name is immediately registered when you incorporate as a limited liability company or a sole proprietorship. Never overlook the possibility of using a DBA (Doing Business As) name.

The registration authorities will vary between states. Locate the appropriate registration authorities in your state.

• Obtain an Employer Identification Number (EIN), if necessary. You must apply for an Employer Identification Number if you aren't a sole owner or an LLC with just one member. Otherwise, the IRS will utilize your personal SSN for tax purposes.

• Comply with additional legal requirements

These can require getting a business license or a seller's permit. The explanation offered below can help you understand more about what goes into that final stage.

• Look over and abide by all applicable legislation.

In addition to choosing a legal structure and establishing your company, there are additional requirements to meet in order to ensure that your business is operating legally. These include getting any necessary business licenses and approvals. There are licensing requirements that are specific to each industry; for instance, if you're launching a construction business, you'll need the required building permits.

Adhering to Legal Requirements

Federal, state, and occasionally even local regulations are applicable to businesses. Verifying the prerequisites for each of those three levels is essential. Your business won't be a legal entity if you don't check every box, so you must.

If necessary, get a seller's license.

Most states need you to apply for a seller's permit if your business offers to sell tangible commodities to the general public as a wholesaler or retailer. The term "tangible property" merely designates material possessions like furniture, equipment, toys, cars, and other building materials. Some regions additionally require service providers including accountants, lawyers, and therapists to obtain a seller's permit.

If you have a seller's permit, you are permitted to charge sales tax to customers. When you fill out the tax payment form, be sure to include the sales tax permit number. The state will then receive payment from you each quarter. You can submit an application for a seller's permit to the Board of Equalization, Franchise Tax Board, or Sales Tax Commission in your state. To help you find the appropriate offices, locate your state. As an alternative, you can look up "seller's permit [state name]" online to find out how to apply at your local office.

Apply for a federal business license if necessary.

Nearly all businesses need some sort of license or permit to operate legally, but the requirements vary, which can be perplexing. Which specific licenses is your business required to have? A significant deciding aspect in this is your industry. For instance, a contractor's license is necessary for construction enterprises.

Get yourself a state license.

The vast majority of states have certain licensing requirements for conducting business out of a warehouse, your home, or even a retail storefront. According to Chase Bank, these may include:

- Operating licenses
- Building permits
- Land-use and zoning permits
- Signage is allowed

Just keep in mind that every state will have different requirements. For example, in Georgia, you need to get an Occupational Tax Certificate (OTC) if you run a physical business, whereas, in New York State, you need a General Vendor License even if you don't. Obtaining and maintaining a professional license.

Certain professions require professional licenses, compared to the federal corporation licenses you need to run a business legally. On the contrary, a license of this kind ensures that you are authorized to provide the services you are advertising.

Double-check the requirements set forth by your state, and keep in mind to renew your license every year.

Recognize your tax obligations as a small business.

Depending on the kind of business entity they establish, entrepreneurs must pay different amounts of precise federal taxes. All businesses, excluding partnerships, are required to file a yearly return for income tax purposes. Partnerships are required to file an information return.

As previously stated, any business that is owned and operated as an LLC or corporation must have an Employer Identification Number (EIN). Even if you operate your business as a sole proprietorship using your SSN, you are liable for self-employment tax.

It's time to decide which taxes, after registration, you'll be responsible for paying. These are the three categories:

Self-Employment Tax (SE Tax)

A person who is an independent contractor, such as a business owner, is required to pay taxes on Social Security and Medicare. For notaries public and other groups, there are particular rules and exceptions.)

Payroll Tax

You are in charge of numerous employment tax duties, such as payments and form submissions, when you have employees.

Excise tax

Excise taxes are a different issue you should consider, depending on the kind of your business, the location where you operate, and other variables. For example, there is a federal excise tax that must be paid on some buses, trucks, and trucks tractors used on public roadways in the United States.

Let's go through what we already know about the rules necessary to start a business.

- Legal Requirements for Starting a Business
- Choose the state in which you will reside.
- Register your business name.
- Apply for an Employer Identification Number (EIN) online.
- Get a seller's permit.
- Get a federal business license.
- Apply for a license with the state.
- Complete and update professional licensing applications.
- Recognize your tax obligations as a small business.

Make a plea for funding

Starting a small business may only need borrowing money from family and friends. However, larger firms will require more investment.

Startup capital is essential regardless of the kind of business you're establishing. Having steady cash will make it possible for you to launch your business more successfully and economically, whether you want to employ loans, grants, or the assistance of loved ones and friends.

Summary

What Are the Conditions for Starting a Business?

A business plan is a document that details the operations and both the short and long-term goals of your business.

Business Name: On all documents and licenses, your name will be used in place of the name of your company.

Business Structure: this outlines the ownership and management philosophies that your organization will use.

Business registration: Your business needs this registration in order to operate legally. This registration is done with the state authorities.

Legal prerequisites. It's possible that you'll also need licenses for business and permissions alongside the initial registration.

Every aspiring business owner wants more money, good leads, and clients. Starting a business, nevertheless, may not be one of those instances when people are going to come when you create it. Take into account your ability to successfully join the market with your product or service and whether the current economic climate is conducive to launching a business. The market, time, and preparation are all crucial factors in getting a new business off the ground.

To create and maintain a successful business, you'll also need to evaluate your finances, complete all the required legal paperwork, choose your partners, research apps for startup development, and choose the best tools and procedures to launch your marketing and sales. Plus a lot more.

Prerequisites for Starting a Business

The following are the requirements for starting a business:

• A seller's permit or other current permits (as well as other legal documents)

• A company name

- A company or ownership structure

- A certificate of business registration

- A source of financing

If you don't have these things in place, you needlessly imperil your brand-new company's future.

Chapter Three

HOW TO FINANCE YOUR BUSINESS

Money is needed for startup costs or business expansion. Depending on your specific business, you can pick from a variety of techniques to raise the needed funds. Leveraging your funds is one of the most common financing methods, although debt financing (taking a loan) and equity funding (selling stock in your business to raise funds) are also very popular. Other creative strategies include using a credit card, crowdfunding, or purchase order financing.

OBTAINING A BUSINESS LOAN

Locate lenders for businesses. Loan finance is arguably the most common technique for financing a business. You agree to repay the borrowed funds over a predetermined time period. The lender makes money by charging interest. The most well-known commercial lenders are as follows:

• Operating banks. If you conduct business with a bank, you can visit them and ask how to get a business loan.

Management of Small Businesses. Despite the fact that it is not legally permitted to do so, the SBA is going to trust loans for small businesses. This suggests that if you go into default, the SBA will pay the bill. Depending on your sector, you might or might not be allowed to describe your business as "small."

• Online lenders. Online lenders often have more lenient loan requirements and won't request collateral from you. However, you need to check the lender's reputation by getting in touch with the Better Business Bureau and a local consumer advocacy group.

Gather the necessary documentation. A lender must assess your company's financial status before approving a loan. Obtain the following paperwork, which is what most lenders require.

• The resumes of the owners and management. Company plans, personal and corporate tax returns over the previous three years, personal and corporate bank records, credit reports, company licenses, articles of organization or incorporation, as well as commercial leases.

Continually update your financial reporting. The majority of lenders will also demand financial details from you. Verify the creation of the following and the updating of the data:

• Personal financial statements that have been attested to by all significant business owners. Typically, a personal financial statement is requested from anyone who owns over twenty percent of the business.

• The balance sheet of a company. This is a summary of your business that includes information about its assets, obligations, and owner equity.

• A declaration of income. This report describes your company's profitability over a specified time period.

• A cash flow analysis. Take a look at your credit report. If your company isn't established, a bank won't lend to it. Instead, they will use your credit history when making a financing choice. Check your credit history and make any necessary corrections before submitting a loan application.

• Common errors include inaccurate balances, inaccurate credit limits, and accounts that are misrepresented as being in collections or default.

• Correct errors to the offending bureau of credit online or in writing. You can use a letter from the Federal Trade Commission as a model.

Obtain pledgeable security. It could be simpler to receive a loan if assets are used as collateral. If you default on the loan, your lender may take the assets. Due to this extra security, banks can request collateral if you do not have a credit history.

• It is acceptable to use a variety of assets as collateral. You could offer valuables like your house, car, equipment, or other goods as a pledge. Consult the banks about the specific criteria.

• Clearly state the condition and value of your collateral. For instance, you could need your collateral to be appraised.

In contrast the loans. After you submit your application, a Lender should decide on it. Usually, it takes two to four weeks to get an answer. If you applied for loans from more than one lender, you should review the loan information:

The interest rate. Find out the loan's annual percentage rate.

• Fees. Other fees, such as an origination fee, might be owed. Read the small print to discover more about the fees assessed.

• Early payment penalties. For the chance to repay your loan early, certain lenders could charge you a fee.

• The duration of repayment. Check the loan's payback schedule. Usually, the longer the loan is outstanding, the lower your monthly payment will be. However, you will end up paying more overall.

Please submit your application. Please fill in the required details and verify their accuracy. If you have any questions, get in touch with the loan officer you have been working with. Send your application and all required supporting documents along with a copy of your documents.

SEEKING OUT INVESTORS

Select the investors you want to court. Selling stakes in ownership in your firm is one way to raise money. Choose who you want to pursue first. There are many different types and sizes of investors.

• Associates. You might choose to enlist a coworker. If so, you can convert your one-man operation into a partnership. Your ideal partner would have the skills you need, such as experience in marketing, product development, or sales.

The general public. Shares of public companies may be purchased by the general public. If this technique appeals to you, you should arrange a meeting with a securities lawyer to discuss your options. The Securities and Exchange Commission must receive a number of paperwork due to the protracted "going public" process.

• Wealthy individuals. Numerous wealthy individuals may make investments in new businesses; these persons are commonly referred to as "angel investors." In exchange, the investor seeks a position on the board of directors or access to daily operations.

Business venture capital firms. Some investors opt to work with venture capital companies, which evaluate companies and choose the ones to invest in. Investments of this nature are active. For its investment, the company would ask for the right to make decisions. Nevertheless, they work together with you to grow the company.

Recognize the benefits and drawbacks of equity financing. After selling a part of your business, you now have an additional shareholder who is eligible to get a share of future profits. They will also likely have voting rights in corporate decisions and full access to your books.

• Based on the sector you operate in, you might need to surrender more than 50% of your company, which would mean losing control. But if your business fails, you won't have to pay them.

• Compare this funding option carefully to your other options. For instance, if you take out a loan, you won't be worrying about a new owner.

Identify prospective investors. Finding potential investors for your company might be challenging. Some investors will only explore opportunities in particular industries, while others won't even consider you except you have already raised six figures yourself. However, you can begin the process by using the methods indicated below to find possible investors:

• Look online. Do a search for "investor" and "name of the sector you work in." Visit their websites to find out more about the businesses they invest in.

• Speak with the local Chamber of Commerce. You might be able to receive leads from the nearby business community. Additionally, the local Small Business Development Center could be able to suggest investors.

• Search the SBIC directory for names. The SBA, which also oversees the Small Business Investment Company program, authorizes private investment funds.

• For business purposes, engage a capital broker. These brokers can introduce you to their contacts in their investor networks. If you need advice choosing a company capital broker, consult your accountant or lawyer.

Create an argumentative presentation. Your business strategy will serve as the primary framework for your presentation. Investors will be able to tell if you have a marketable product or service and are well-positioned to grow. But a compelling presentation will go beyond the scope of your business strategy.

• Make sure you can succinctly describe your business. You will consider what makes your business unique as a result of this endeavor, despite how challenging it may be.

• Research potential investors. Try to get to know the investor on a personal level within the first five minutes.

• Promote your products and services. If you make the things, bring a sample to show the investor. Create a little movie that showcases your services if you provide them. Ensure that the investor can actually see your business in action.

Exercise due diligence. Every business that potential investors are considering supporting is carefully scrutinized. As a result, during the due diligence process, the investor will carefully review your service, product, market, and management team.

• Depending on the magnitude of the potential investment, you might wish to consult a lawyer when performing your due diligence.

• If what they see interests them, they will prepare a document explaining the terms of their financial commitment.

MORE CHOICE

Obtain money to pay for purchasing orders.

If you resell things to pay your suppliers, you might need a loan. Large orders, in particular, may require more financial outlays on your part. When a purchase order is funded, the finance department will pay the supplier directly.

• This type of financing is only viable if your markup is sufficiently high. It must have a gross profit margin of at least 30%.

• Contact a finance company to find out more information about this type of funding.

Use your bills as collateral for a loan

The practice of "factoring" involves getting an advance on your payments in order to raise money. If your clients are slow to pay, factoring can provide you with the funds you require. Approximately 80% of the invoice's value can be paid to you immediately away. When your client finally makes a payment, you get the balance less any fees.

• You will only be qualified if your customers have acceptable credit. For example, reputable government or commercial clients are first-rate.

• Do your research before working with a factoring service. Ask them about their experience and find out if they work with businesses of your size. Check to determine whether there is a minimum that has to be considered.

Ask friends or family for a loan

People that are familiar with you could be prepared to offer you money so that you can finance your business. This is unquestionably the greatest option if you only require a small amount of borrowed funds.

• Behave toward your family as you would a bank. Describe your financial needs and your repayment strategies.

• Consider providing your lender with interest payments. Furthermore, it will show that you are sincere and not merely seeking a little extra money for luxuries.

• Create and sign a proforma. If you do this, you are going to be legally obligated to give the money back.

Withdraw money from your retirement account

You can finance a new or existing firm using an old employer's IRA or 401(k). Your present investments must be moved into a retirement plan created especially for the business. The money is then used by the plan to purchase corporate stock. You should ask a financing business for help because this is a challenging process. To find out if it has a monthly fee for advice, look at the company's prices. Before using your retirement money to finance your business, thoroughly weigh your possibilities. To assist you after retirement, some money was set aside. If your business collapses, you'll lose these savings.

Make a credit card payment

Depending on how much money you need, you can decide to use a credit card. It's a great option if you can obtain a credit card with an introductory 0% rate for a year or more. Remember the following credit card advice:

• Be sure to submit an application for a business credit card. You should not blend your personal and business expenses. Combining them will give the impression that your business isn't really a separate entity, which could be problematic if you want to operate as an LLC or corporation.

Please use the card responsibly. It's usually not a smart idea to use a credit card for large purchases like equipment. Instead, choose an equipment loan. Instead, pay for immediate responsibilities like travel expenses with your credit card.

Use crowdfunding to raise money

One-time endeavors like writing a screenplay or making a rap album are eligible for funding. Visitors to the website can make donations to your project once you register there.

• Crowdfunding shouldn't be utilized for continuing, continuous fundraising; it should only be used for short-term projects. Peerbackers, RocketHub, and Indiegogo are a few well-known crowdfunding websites. Explore their websites to become familiar with their policies.

Request a home equity loan. Your house can be your most valuable possession. Therefore, banks will give you a loan if you use your house as collateral for the loan. You can get a home equity loan or a Home Equity Line Of Credit (HELOC) to fund your business.

• You get a lump sum when you take out a home equity loan, and you pay it back in equal monthly installments. In comparison, a HELOC works like a credit card. You have to pay it back once you've used it all.

• Speak with a lender to learn the terms of obtaining a home equity loan or a HELOC. Examine loan conditions, interest rates, and the time period needed to repay the loan.

• As a first option, you shouldn't use your residence as collateral. If your business doesn't succeed, you'll lose your house.

Investigate grants

You may be qualified to receive a grant from the federal, state, or local governments. A few nonprofits also give money to businesses. Grants for emerging technologies are routinely given, however, they are typically only accessible to specialized businesses. Grants are typically not a smart choice for businesses. Conversely, if you think you might qualify, find out about funding options via your local business development office. You can get money via personal savings, business grants, and loans.

Chapter Four

YOU
AND ENTREPRENEURSHIP

Are you ready to begin a life of entrepreneurship? The best guidance for thriving in your small business sector is offered here.

• Create a plan for attracting customers.

Once your new business has been officially established with the government and all necessary paperwork has been completed, how do you go about obtaining clients? The reality is that a fledgling company must build interest in its product or service even before it is ready to ship. To spread awareness, you can use a variety of tools and techniques. So, where do you even start?

Your target market is a crucial consideration. You won't be able to draw in customers if you don't know who they are. One of the first questions you need to ask yourself is who wants what I'm delivering. Who might gain from it? Who would love it? To create a successful customer acquisition strategy, your target demography must be as well specified as possible.

• Identify your target audience.

To find out who your target audience is and what kind of messaging would resonate with them, you must conduct research on them. By employing research, surveys, and interviews, learn about their backgrounds, passions, goals, and challenges.

Their age, daily activities, and the social media networks they use are all relevant information. And a whole lot more.

Making very specific consumer personas could greatly improve your efforts to attract new clients. Read this guide that includes adjustable buyer persona templates for establishing buyer personas. After selecting one or more customer personas, print them out, hang them on your wall, and take into account their requirements before making any business-related decisions.

DEVELOPING A BRAND IDENTITY

When starting a business, you please must research your target market and lay the foundation for a strong brand identity. Your company's brand identity reflects your values, your communication style, and the emotions you want customers to experience when doing business with you. If you employ a consistent brand identity to market your business, you will look more expert and be able to attract more clients.

• Boost your online visibility.

Once you've determined your target audience and created your brand identity, you can begin creating your small business's fundamental marketing tools, such as your blog, website, email tool, social media profiles, and conversion tool. To acquire more in-depth information on these topics, see our introduction to small business marketing here.

• Generate and nurture leads.

Once you've started building your online presence and spreading the word about your business, you need to generate the leads which will eventually turn into customers. Lead generation is the process of attracting and converting potential customers and clients into leads. By building a strong lead generation engine, you can keep your sales funnel full of prospects even when you're not around.

• Establish a framework for your sales.

If you take the effort to set up your sales process correctly from the start, you may be able to avoid the agonizing problems that come with missing data in the future. Use a CRM, or customer relationship management system, to keep track of all of your current and prospective customers. A CRM is a central database. There are many options, but you ought to take small business-focused CRMs into consideration. Excel is not a part of this!

ESTABLISHING YOUR SALES GOALS

Don't let sales jargon like ROI and KPIs scare you. All of this basically implies that you must ascertain what you need in order to thrive and grow, including how much money you need and how many products you must sell to get there.

• Work with a salesperson.

It may be alluring to manage every facet of your brand-new company by yourself, even sales. But if you want to scale, you must hire your first salesperson; you require a full-time employee who will work to comprehend your buyer and then sell to them. When employing your first salesperson, experience in actual sales and familiarity with your company's target market should be given more weight than seniority. The establishment of your sales development team will therefore require a strategy.

• increase the yield from your sales efforts.

Efficiency is the key. Develop a sales process that works well for businesses of all sizes by using a structure like this practical step sales process. Furthermore, you ought to automate data entry tasks for sales or set up notifications for any time a potential customer takes action. By doing this, you may spend less time looking through records and calling the wrong prospects and instead concentrate more on strategy and actual selling.

• Work to please your customers.

Getting new customers is important, but maintaining them is just as important. Once customers have made a purchase from your business, you shouldn't ignore them; rather, you must take care of them, offer them top-notch customer service, and motivate them to recommend your business to others.

Even while inbound marketing and sales are crucial to your funnel, the process doesn't end there. In fact, if you can't keep your customers satisfied, all of the time and effort you invest into refining your strategy in those areas are going to be for naught.

This suggests that the foundation of your company should be developing a model for customer success. Think about the various channels social media, web aggregators, and product reviews use to spread the word about your services.

To be fair, they are all quick and effective. A significant chunk of your prospects is evaluating your company based on the information and resources that other people are disseminating about your brand, even if you have control over it and can improve your marketing and sales playbooks.

REACTING QUICKLY TO CUSTOMER ISSUES

People anticipate swift response times (some swifter than others depending on the channel), hence it's crucial to be quick as well as effective to keep up with demands so that you're consistently providing outstanding service to avoid losing clients' trust.

Keep track of how often different outlets reference your company. Whether it's on a social network or somewhere else, find out where your customers tend to spend the most time and pose the most questions, and then engage them there.

Keep track of every interaction you have with a specific consumer.

The finest advice for interactions with your clients comes from context. Keep track of the outcomes of every connection you've had with certain customers because knowing how they've interacted with your company in the past will be useful in the future.

When did they first become one of your clients? Do they have any prior sales experience? What amount of money did they spend? Have they endorsed or denounced your products or customer service? Possessing the responses to these questions might enable you to present a more comprehensive picture when responding to queries and conversing with clients.

Create feedback mechanisms.

As soon as you have your first customer, you should actively solicit their insights. As your company grows, this will become more challenging, but remember that your staff members who interact with consumers are an invaluable source of information because they are closest to your current and potential clients.

Make sure your website has a FAQ area.

Scale this program as you grow and provide your customers with the tools they need to take care of themselves. This could initially appear to be a simple FAQ page. Make your website a resource for your growing consumer base so they can self-serve as it grows over time. You may, for instance, turn your FAQ page into a library or knowledge base that offers guidance and/or addresses frequently asked issues.

Chapter Five

ACQUIRING NEW CUSTOMERS

Learn how to draw in new customers and capitalize on your current ones if you want to grow your business. You must make an investment in a customer acquisition plan if you want to draw in the right leads for your company and increase the likelihood that you will be able to retain them over time.

In this chapter, you'll discover the principles of customer acquisition, how to cut down on the cost of acquiring new consumers, and how to maximize the value of your current clientele. By the time you're done, you'll be able to create an acquisition strategy that is flexible enough to withstand shifting market conditions and trends.

What does the term "customer acquisition" mean?

Customer acquisition is the process whereby you persuade potential customers to buy your products or hire your service. An effective lead generation strategy:

71

1) Attracts leads;

2) Nurtures leads until they are prepared to convert into sales; and

3) Converts leads into clients. The total cost of these actions (CAC) is your client acquisition cost.

Why is attracting new clients crucial?

All sizes and ages of businesses must find clients. It helps your company to:

• Produce revenue to pay bills, pay employees, and reinvest in expansion; and

• Offer evidence of success to entice partners, investors, and influencers from other sources.

Investors are happy when companies can regularly attract and convert new customers.

What is achieved through client acquisition?

Customer acquisition is the process of finding a repeatable, systematic plan to attract clients to your business. You may wait for customers to come to you on their own, but doing so won't guarantee that your profits will increase or even remain constant over time.

Customer acquisition experts use specific strategies to persuade potential customers to take action. This process aims to create a rigorous, long-term strategy for attracting new customers and boosting sales for the business.

In many ways, this approach is similar to marketing because you look for chances to market your business and cultivate relationships with customers. But there is a difference between the two.

DEVELOPMENT OF CUSTOMERS VERSUS MARKETING

While marketing aims to raise awareness, customer acquisition aims to motivate action. Think about placing a Facebook advertisement, for instance, for your intended audience. Analytics can be used to gauge the success of your campaign by counting the number of people who have interacted with it, shared it, or commented on it. Advertising that.

Acquisition refers to what happens once potential customers click through to your page or receive your emails. When a customer chooses to purchase your goods or services, you have acquired that customer. Put simply? Marketing raises brand recognition while acquisition boosts revenue.

You may now be asking what sets lead generation apart from customer acquisition.

Let's analyze it.

THE CUSTOMER ACQUISITION FUNNEL

To depict the customer journey in the business sector, a funnel or other equivalent image that highlights the steps in the process of purchasing and the strategic thinking of the prospect is widely employed.

As they move through the funnel, customers who become buyers:

• Raise brand awareness;

• Add your offering to their list of prospective purchases;

• Decide to spend money doing business with you.

To simplify the process, lead generation, lead acquisition, and lead conversion frequently take place at the top, middle, and bottom of the funnel, respectively.

The phrase "client acquisition" is also frequently used to describe the complete funnel.

Here is another, less funnel-like way of thinking about it:

In the example before, the "attract," "convert," and "close" phases are when prospective customers are drawn in and persuaded to become paying customers.

In certain firms, the middle and top of the marketing funnel combine lead generation with customer acquisition. This is due to the fact that moving customers down the funnel frequently requires more specialized, customized strategies, such as sales leads and closing methods.

In this book, "customer acquisition" refers to the entire funnel.

PAID MARKETING

Acquisition marketing is the process of creating an advertising and marketing campaign that specifically targets consumers who are already considering your products and services. Because they are already familiar with your brand, these clients make excellent conversion candidates.

Acquisition marketing stands out from other types of advertising because it concentrates on clients who already have knowledge of your business's existence and are considering making a purchase.

Marketing for online purchase

Utilizing online channels including display ads, social media, and organic search, digital acquisition marketing aims to attract and target new customers. A successful digital strategy for acquisition frequently requires collaboration and alignment between both customer service and marketing teams.

Your marketing staff develops and disseminates fresh marketing materials that may catch the attention of prospective customers. Your customer service representatives, on the other hand, are the ones who have a direct line to your current clients, and these customers maybe some of your best marketers.

Visitors to your website will read the articles passively that your advertising staff have written and may decide to buy your products. But if they utilize the live chat function on your website, visitors will speak with a representative of your customer service staff immediately.

Or, if a prospective client gets in touch with you via social media, they're going to probably interact with a customer service representative.

Simply said, your customer service team is just as effective at attracting and keeping new customers as your marketing team. Acquisition marketing, therefore, goes outside the purview of your marketing division.

Before we address upkeep through your customer care team, let's first talk about various client acquisition tactics that your marketers may employ to spark interest in prospective customers and convert them.

ACQUISITION TECHNIQUES

Businesses use organic search, email, and organic social media as platforms to market their goods and services to potential new clients. The most effective acquisition strategy for your company will be determined by the target market, the resources at hand, and the overall plan.

Paid and free, inbound and outbound, among other types of customer acquisition tactics, are among the available options.

Organic Results

SERPS from Google or Bing are examples of search engine results pages (SERPs), often known as "organic search." By extension, all of your attempts to rank higher in these results are included in organic search marketing.

If you want to leverage organic search as a channel for attracting customers, you must engage in search engine optimization (SEO). Similar to social media, SEO helps content marketing campaigns by increasing the accessibility of your content to your target audience.

Think about this When you Google something, you often select one of the top results, right? In order to get users to click on your material, it must rank highly on search engine results pages.

Fortunately, there's no need to rely on educated estimates when using organic search to support client acquisition efforts. Using tools like Open Site Explorer, SEMRush, and Ahrefs, which can likewise be utilized to create interesting content that attracts potential new customers, you can discover the ideal keywords for your organization.

Pay-Per-Click

On search engines, pay-per-click, or PPC, advertising is a type of paid search marketing. Additionally, you can use PPC networks like Google advertising to run display advertising on publisher and affiliate websites.

Rather than optimizing your content organically, PPC lets you create a search result and pay for it to show up alongside organic results, increasing your chances of being discovered by searchers. For the best performance in search engine results, optimize your content and advertisements using tools like Microsoft Advertising and Google Keyword Planner.

Platforms on organic social media

Social media marketing comes in two flavors: free and paid. The best ways to use natural social media are to build brand awareness, give your business a personality, and share content that is already available elsewhere, like your blog or videos. Consider it as fuel for a fire if you've already started using other acquisition strategies.

Organic social media additionally capitalizes on most of the virality effect by encouraging your clients and followers to share the news about you.

Paid-for Social Media

Depending on your financial capacity and target market, adopting paid social media platforms may be a better option for your business. Spending money on social media visibility and advertisements is a surefire way to reach your audience without having to build up a following of ardent fans. (But don't get me wrong, that's also important.)

Organize and schedule your social networking content using this free calendar template and management tool.

Sponsored posts gather user data like names and email addresses from their audience rather than merely delivering your content before the relevant individuals. Facebook Lead Ads enable social media promotion. If your firm is looking to increase its list, this might serve as the acquisition approach for you since this information can differentiate between a lead and a follower.

Email: What do marketers do with each piece of customer data they acquire from various means of client acquisition? To communicate with and convert their customers, firms develop an email list and make use of that list as a marketing tool.

Although email marketing might seem to be a dated way of customer acquisition, it is an extremely effective strategy for keeping in the know about your audience and offering excellent content, product information, discounts, and events. Email is also an excellent way to interact with your target market, whether you're emailing a note of appreciation for a message on a birthday or an enlightening marketing email.

Contrary to the likes of search, social media, or content marketing, email marketing offers you a direct connection to your customers' inboxes. Marketing via email is the most effective customer acquisition method available aside from direct sales due to the fact that it directly meets each customer's demands.

Referrals

Occasionally, the most effective source of tested customer acquisition tactics is right before you—your very own consumers. Among the most efficient techniques to attract new consumers is via gaining customer references. While you cannot force your current clients to suggest you to others as well, there are a few things you can do to encourage them to do so.

Establishing a referral program is a surefire approach to obtaining more customers to recommend you. Offering benefits, whether in the form of credit, tangible gifts, or monetary awards (and compensating them in return), is usually the most effective technique for encouraging a consumer to spread the news about your brand. If you value a client reference highly for your business, you must trade it for something of comparable worth.

For B2C firms, a structured, incentive-based program frequently works well, whereas B2B businesses may have greater success directly seeking customer referrals. Whatever referral program you choose, ensure to first offer value before presenting inquiries. Give your customers a cause to suggest you; once they are pleased with your products or services, they have no choice but to inform others about you.

Events

Events like conferences, webinars, and trade shows are wonderful ways to meet potential clients and acquire new business.

Because most events these days are done online, it may be easier to gain clients because participants must sign up with their email addresses (whether they pay or not). Meeting prospects face to face does not always make gathering this information easy or natural.

Furthermore, virtual events are a great method to meet prospective customers and sponsors from the comfort of your own home. If you haven't previously employed this strategy for customer acquisition, consider holding a virtual summit, or webinar, or renting a booth at a larger event.

Conventional Marketing

Traditional advertising avenues like TV, radio, and print media work effectively for small businesses as well as large corporations with the funding to launch multi-city campaigns. Traditional marketing can be a useful tool for attracting new clients if you target your ads wisely and consider the audiences that each publisher serves.

In most cases, you can find out more about the audience in the publisher's media buying guide. They will also specify the permitted size and any other requirements for advertising or publishing there.

Let's talk about a few potential channels for the customer acquisition strategy before moving on to some specific strategies that fall under the jurisdiction of each channel.

MARKETING STRATEGIES

Techniques for attracting new clients

SEO, content marketing, gated content, social media advertising, blogging, product cost, video promotion, advertisement, email retargeting, and client highlights. To reach the intended result, you may mix a number of strategies while creating a customer acquisition plan.

Search engine optimization, or SEO

A channel for client acquisition is organic search.

Despite the fact that SEO is not an exact science, there are a number of tried-and-true methods that can raise the position of your content in organic search results. SEO best practices include producing indexable material, or content that can be read, understood, and indexed by search engines inside a SERP. Your post's "indexability" can be raised by:

• Ensuring that your main keyword appears in the post title;

- Providing alt text for your photographs.

- Making online transcriptions of video and audio content

- Your website's internal links

These are some foundations to get you started, however, there are numerous elements that affect SEO.

Several factors make SEO a popular method for attracting new customers: It is very simple and inexpensive. 64% of marketers actively invest in SEO recently as SEO becomes a priority for more marketing teams globally. Your content is going to rank higher than it did earlier if you put the time into researching SEO strategies, staying current with industry developments, and improving your blog posts.

CONTENT MARKETING

A channel for client acquisition is organic search.

Content marketing is an effective strategy for attracting new clients for many different types of businesses. Making new, engaging, and pertinent material is a very effective way to grab your audience's attention and lead them to your website.

When it pertains to content marketing, there is no wrong kind of material you may create. The heart of content marketing is making a connection with and converting your audience. Every single bit of content you produce must therefore be relevant to your audience and contain a clear call to action. Content marketing also includes the creation of content and its promotion.

MARKETING ON SOCIAL MEDIA

Both free and paid social media are outlets for consumer acquisition.

Without a solid strategy, using social media may require a lot of effort for little reward.

• Which social media platforms should you stay away from?

• How will your social brand be voiced, and which members of your marketing team are going to be in charge of overseeing and producing content?

• Do you have a crisis strategy in place?

If these questions seem intimidating, don't be concerned. Organic social media sharing might sometimes seem like screaming into thin air. Having a well-defined audience is essential for getting access to the right networks.

BLOGGING

Organic Search is a method of attracting new clients.

Blogging is a highly suggested acquisition method for companies of all sizes, across all industries, and with a variety of audiences. By maintaining a blog, you are able to explore a range of topics, show off your knowledge of your industry, and gain the trust of your readers. Furthermore, blogging constantly gives you new opportunities to engage with your audience, whether it be through an image they are able to save for later, a comment they can reply to, or a tempting button they can click.

Before you make the choice to create a blog, be sure you have resources that are sustainable at your disposal. Dedicated employees, independent contractors, or site visitors can all contribute to your blog. If you have a visual artist and editor on staff, it may be simpler to make sure that your content is optimized for both search engines and reader experience. Last but not least, adding a blog to the website is quite easy depending on your hosting platform.

PRODUCT PRICING

Your product's pricing strategy is another effective customer-acquisition strategy that may be marketed through any media, including TV advertisements and word-of-mouth marketing. You could also let the cost of your product do all of the marketing for you. It is particularly effective when your competitors' prices are much higher or when they don't employ your pricing approach at all.

For instance, selling freemium software can help you attract customers to whom you can then make upsells. "Free tools" will appeal to those with little resources or those who want to test out your products before subscribing.

If you sell consumer items, "Buy One, Get One Free" will have a flurry of customers clicking "Add to basket," growing your customer base without much effort.

You might consider the following specific pricing strategies:

• Promotional pricing, discount pricing, and freemium pricing

VIDEO MARKETING

The three types of social media are paid search, paid social media, and organic social media.

Making videos is easier than you might believe since higher-quality cameras are becoming more affordable and because there are so many available freelancers. Video is one of the most challenging sorts of media to create. The secret to effective marketing using videos as a component of a bigger content strategy is quality content.

You can outsource any or all of the common video production tasks—including script writing, production, editing, and animation—to freelancers or production firms. Since videos are often the most expensive content types, save your finest ideas for future videos.

The truth is that this type of information is extremely flexible. Social media posts, both those that are purchased and those that are produced naturally on the site, can be used to advertise. Additionally, you may add videos to your website pages and blog posts to boost reader interest and your chances of making a sale.

Not having enough money for video marketing? If your goal is to just assist your audience in visualizing an idea, you can create a Slideshare as an alternative to a video.

SPONSORED OR ADVERTISEMENT-FREE CONTENT

Traditional advertising, paid social media, and sponsored search are all methods for attracting clients.

Sponsored advertising includes things like paid listings on search engine results pages and social media posts from influencers. No matter which medium you use, sponsored adverts can help you get the word out about your products and services and attract new clients. You can experiment with a variety of sponsored content types, such as paid blog posts on pertinent websites, sponsored product mentions, and sponsored search results.

RETARGETING EMAIL

Another channel for acquiring new customers is email.

There is more to email marketing than just the messages you send. Monitoring list behavior and modifying your email remarketing as necessary is also advantageous. For instance, it's reasonable to assume that when you sign up a new subscriber, they are curious about your company and want to learn more. If they don't respond to your initial emails, you should switch up your strategy and A/B test other calls to action.

By watching which links your consumers open in your emails, you can learn what interests them the most. Additionally, subscribers whom entirely unsubscribe could provide you with insight into how your subscribers feel about your emails and the information you offer.

REVIEWS FROM CUSTOMERS (REFERRALS)

New customers frequently come through consumer referrals.

What constitutes a fruitful customer acquisition plan? Gaining the support of your satisfied consumers. Here's how to let your customers promote your business and save you time and money by forgoing more traditional methods of acquisition.

• Request customer reviews. Encourage your customers to share their own accounts of how they learned about your business and why they like it, whether through interviews, user-generated content, case studies, reviews, or other kinds of user-generated content. Give your customers the opportunity to gush about your company on social media or through sponsored advertising.

• Make sharing content easy. Although having a positive outlook can help you get your point across, wouldn't it be preferable if your customers could simply share the content you've created, such as blog posts, images, or social network postings?

The viral loop occurs when your customers share content that motivates their followers to come back to your establishment. Make sure that each piece of content you post has options for sharing via social media and email, and make Click to Tweet buttons in order that your customers can quickly share social updates. A convenient offer will be accepted more frequently by your clients.

All Channels for Gated Content Customer Acquisition

You can gate eBooks, white papers, manuals, templates, and other sorts of content. Because the content generation process is more difficult, some content offers are gated, requiring viewers to exchange sensitive information like names and emails in order to access the content.

Because gated information may be provided through any medium, it can be utilized in combination with pretty much any client acquisition strategy. For example, you may advertise the content on social media or make the landing page search-engine friendly.

Gated content is an essential client acquisition strategy that ranks above SEO, content promotion, and CRO. It might help your blog and content marketing strategy produce more leads. The material needs to be legitimately gated in order to prevent the e-book or guide from being legitimately indexed and searchable online. Otherwise, potential customers won't give you their email and will simply check it out on their own.

It is clear that these customer acquisition tactics work best together. For instance, SEO-optimized content with a call to action to join an email list can be promoted using social media. Despite being a tad wordy, the idea is obvious.

By comparing and contrasting a variety of client acquisition techniques, you may gain more insight into your audience and introduce novel ideas to your current plan. When creating marketing strategies, you should always leave room for research, advancement, and adjustment because you never know when customers will stop engaging with them or stop making purchases from you.

HOW TO MONITOR CLIENT DEVELOPMENT

A trendy term is customer acquisition cost, or CAC as it is more generally known. Customer acquisition cost (CAC), which includes costs for marketing, events, and advertising, is the price to acquire a new customer or client for your business. It is often calculated for a specific campaign or time frame.

CAC is significant because it offers your marketing efforts real value and enables you to determine your ROI, a number that CEOs, managers, and investors all worry about.

HOW TO CALCULATE THE COST TO ACQUIRE

CUSTOMERS

The high-level customer acquisition cost of a campaign is calculated by dividing its marketing costs by the total number of customers it attracted.

ACC FORMULA

The formula for calculating customer acquisition cost (CAC) is $CAC = MC / CA$. Marketing costs are MC. The acquisition of customers is CA.

In order to present a more complete and accurate picture of CAC, you must take into account all costs associated with marketing expenditures, including campaign costs, marketing salaries, and the price of the supplies used to produce those lengthy contracts.

Because it can be a variable metric, the CAC ought not to be the main indicator used to evaluate marketing activity. Why? The following variables could have an impact on the use and worth of your CAC:

• On average, how often do your customers purchase from you? A Starbucks and an Audi shop have drastically different CACs.

• Does/did your company invest money in long-term marketing plans that are predicted to be successful? Consider funding a campaign in Q3 and paying for it in Q1. With that expense, you could not see any new clients right away, which would affect your Q1 CAC.

Regardless, CAC is an important number to calculate (and keep computing) as you add new clients and employ cutting-edge acquisition techniques.

HOW TO LOWER CUSTOMER ACQUISITION COSTS

Here is a simple marketing truth: One can always get better. You can always increase your customer base, boost your marketing, and reduce costs while doing so.

Your perspective will determine whether or not this is good news for you. It's never too late to learn new things or make improvements. Better still, you are not compelled to utilize a subpar indicator that irks management or investors.

If you wish to minimize your CAC, use any of the following tactics to lower the cost of acquiring new customers:

• *Improve your website conversion marketing initiatives.* The effectiveness of your landing pages should be increased, your calls-to-action should be improved, and your copywriting should be polished. Also, make sure your website is mobile and tablet compatible. Consider A/B testing the homepage or shopping cart to see whether the design or copywriting approach performs the best. These will ensure that any current customer acquisition techniques you employ are working as effectively as possible.

• *Boost the value of your current clientele.* This can include launching a brand-new item or improvement that your customers can also purchase. Users' value might increase when they refer new customers to you or just advocate your business.

• *Adjust and enhance your consumer acquisition strategy.* Spend some time designing your acquisition concept and figuring out how much each strategy will cost. Where could you cut back on staffing or additional marketing spending? As costs for specific channels can rise over time, you can always lower CAC by making investments in new, less expensive channels. This process also ensures that your strategy is adaptable and takes into account the most current marketing trends.

HOW TO IMPROVE YOUR MARKETING STRATEGY TO ATTRACT CUSTOMERS

Whether your business has 5 or 1000 employees, developing a strategy for customer acquisition is a smart move because every company needs new customers to grow and prosper. Here are a few things you can do to develop a strong customer acquisition roadmap.

First, make your plan sustainable.

A sustainable client acquisition approach is one that will be effective over the long run. This means that any sort of investment you make, whether they be in terms of resources like money, time, or people, may be sustained into the foreseeable future.

For example, if you intend to use a blog to draw in more customers, you need to be equipped with the resources and tools required to ensure that the content you publish is useful beyond just one or two pieces and continues to generate organic traffic for months, years, or even weeks. As a result, inbound marketing is effective since it consistently drives visitors and, as a result, a steady stream of new customers. Contrast this with commercials, which can work well for attracting customers if they are active.

Add adaptability

Given the ongoing changes in marketing, sales, and consumer behavior, a flexible strategy for client acquisition is especially crucial. As in the past, salespeople are no more the sole source of product information.

The claims made by brands and by businesses or their representatives regarding a product are being questioned by consumers more and more. If you devised a customer acquisition plan that just relied on salesmen, your company would be in trouble. If you maintain your strategy adaptable, you will continually be able to change it to suit shifting market conditions.

Determine who your target market is.

Not every customer is your best customer, therefore if your efforts to acquire new customers aren't focused on the right people, they can end up being a waste of time and money. Before spending money on any client acquisition techniques, you must define your target market.

By simply developing your buyer persona, you may cut out any inefficient or unnecessary acquisition efforts and become more aware of certain wants or tastes that some channels may be able to accommodate. It's important to take a step back and establish a targeted customer acquisition strategy if you want to make the best choices for your business, resources, and audience. Then, you might expect to see actual results from your customer-acquisition efforts.

Modify your approach

Do you understand the term "cross-pollination"? It happens when bees spread pollen among different plants, resulting in species variations that are better equipped to withstand time and the elements. Marketers are like these brave bees in this situation. By diversifying your acquisition strategy and employing a range of acquisition approaches, you boost your chances of connecting with new audiences and generating new leads.

In addition, diversifying your lead generation strategy strikes a balance between risk and reward, making it easier to switch spending to a different, higher-performing strategy if one channel starts to falter.

Monitor each customer's lifetime value

It's important to attract new customers, but it's even more important to keep them as customers over the long term. Knowing which types of consumers have the highest levels of customer loyalty can help you improve your entire strategy and the success of your customer acquisition efforts.

Customer lifetime value is the anticipated net profit that an individual or business will deliver during the course of their relationship as a paying customer. It's a helpful thing to keep in mind as you learn more about your customers and how they interact with your business. It also provides a detailed evaluation of your marketing as well as encourages efforts and has an impact on all business decisions.

Despite being more expensive to acquire, clients with high LTV outperform other clients in terms of revenue, recommendations, and feedback.

Calculating customer LTV is challenging even though a few important factors along the path, including the average sales price and frequency, are not. Regardless of whether you have to make an informed guess at these numbers, having a strong client LTV can assist you in determining how much money a customer will contribute throughout their relationship with your business. By measuring customer LTV with CAC, businesses may calculate how long it takes to recover each investment made in acquiring new customers. They may now deploy their acquisition budget more effectively as a result.

Chapter Six

BUSINESS ONLINE

Starting an online business is an intriguing and affordable way to make additional money or start a new profession. Success in business, though, may be difficult as well. To increase your chances of success, create a business strategy for your online venture. After that, complete the necessary paperwork and set up your website. The last step is to approach potential clients with your goods or services.

Writing a Business Plan

Choose the products or services that your business will provide. Consider your specific abilities, background, and/or experience. Then, think about how you may employ these skills to offer a product or service to your potential customers.

• Consider, for instance, that you are an expert graphic designer and have web design experience. With these skills, you may start your own web design business.

Advice: Consider whether you want to work exclusively online or make tangible products like crafts or artwork when deciding what products or services to provide.

Determine how much time you can spend on your business each day. Prior to starting your business, choose if you want it to be your full-time or part-time job. Then, consider how much time you have available each day to dedicate to the business. Consider how long it will take for the products or services you are going to provide to be successful as well.

• Since it will undoubtedly take some time for your business to succeed, starting it part-time may be suitable. Some businesses may be more flexible than others. For instance, certain jobs, such as consulting, may require you to work around the needs of the client, whilst other jobs, such as working as a freelance web developer or selling crafts, may allow you to work whenever you please.

Research the market for your good or service to see if there is a need for it. Analyze the size of your possible rivals and educate yourself on the newest developments in the market you want to enter. It is also beneficial to survey your target market over the phone or in person to ascertain whether they would be interested in what you have to offer. You can then assess if your business can fill a market need as a result.

• For instance, you might get in touch with nearby businesses to inquire about their interest in hiring a freelance marketer to handle their social media accounts.

• You may put on a product you're selling at a local market or among individuals you think would have interested in it to see how people react to it.

• Even though it is not necessary to undertake marketing research before starting a business, doing so can increase your success rates.

Make sure your products and services are suitable for an internet store. Not every business can run a home office or operate online. You may not be able to run your firm from home, for instance, if it necessitates heavy production or client meetings. Some businesses, like the ones described below, can, nevertheless, be easily run from home:

• Blogging; accounting; graphic design; web design; financial management

• Promote your original artwork, jewelry, and handmade goods.

• Creating gift baskets; consulting; and offering writing and editing services.

• Engaging in online assistant work

Create a budget for the start-up and expansion of your business. The expenditures involved in starting your business will vary greatly depending on the specific sort of business being offered. For instance, if you wanted to operate a home-based online bookstore, you would need to purchase inventory. A service-based business can require less initial financing as a substitute. Determine how much money you'll need to invest in the materials your business will require. Additionally, there are a few typical costs that are typical of online businesses and that you should include in your budget:

• Website hosting – Your business probably needs a website. Web hosting services guarantee the availability of your website. They normally charge a small monthly fee depending on the technical support they offer and the size of your site.

• Website design – Whether you select an expensive template, build the site from scratch, or hire a designer, the cost of this service varies. A basic website can be created by you or using a template for less than $100, although a designer might charge between $100 and $5,000.

• Online shopping cart – You'll need one for your customers to utilize if you offer products and services that can be purchased online. You might be able to discover a service that only costs when you complete a transaction, even though many providers charge $5 per month.

Building an email mailing list is crucial for selling your goods and bringing in money.

• Materials costs – If you're selling a product, these costs include the cost of the raw materials and any production equipment. If you are offering a service, such as application or assistance services, this applies to those as well.

• Website security and maintenance – you'll need to regularly update your website, which could result in extra costs. Additionally, you might need to spend more money to secure your client's data, particularly if you're handling payments.

Put together a business plan. A plan is necessary for every business, no matter how little, since it will help you stay on track to meet your goals. Every facet of your business is covered in your business plan, including the following:

• *Business idea:* Describe the organizational structure of your company and the products or services it will offer. Include a succinct description of your company's market.

• *Area research:* Find out who the key competitors are in the area you are entering, as well as who your target market is and what they need.

• *Marketing strategy:* Outline your intended approach to your market, customer interactions, and method of distribution.

• *Operations plan:* Specify your everyday operations, including the steps involved in producing your product or service.

• *Financial plan:* Describe your company's financing strategy, the costs you expect to incur, and the revenue you expect to bring in.

SETTING UP AN ONLINE BUSINESS ACCOUNT

Determine the legal form of your business. This will have an impact on how you file your taxes as well as how much you are owing. The majority of small businesses are sole proprietorships since they require the least amount of paperwork to get up and operate. An attorney who specializes in Internet law could be able to assist you with the best choice if you are considering employing a different form of legal structure.

• One-person business — A sole proprietorship makes no distinction between the owner and the business in terms of the law. You are therefore responsible for the company's gains, losses, commitments, and deeds. It's easy to choose this option for a home-based business.

• Partnership – A partnership is defined as when two or more persons share ownership. Normally, a lawyer is used to negotiate a partnership agreement. The company's obligations are entirely the responsibility of each individual partner, while profits, losses, and liabilities are equally divided. You might choose a partnership if you want to work with another person.

• LLC – Limited Liability Company – Choose a name for your LLC, and then pay your state's filing fee to submit your articles of organization. Owners of LLCs are not personally liable for the choices and actions of the company, but they are still required to file individual income tax returns and pay self-employment tax on the earnings they make.

• Corporation – Owned by shareholders, a corporation is a distinct legal entity. Select a company name for your corporation, then send the documents of incorporation to your state for registration. You'll also need to register with the IRS and get a tax ID. Separate tax returns are filed by corporations and their owners. If you want to know if this kind of business will benefit you, you should speak with an accountant or lawyer. Typically, smaller businesses shouldn't adopt this structure.

• S Corporation – Like a typical corporation, this independent legal entity is owned by shareholders, but to avoid double taxation, profits, and losses are handed through to the owners' individual tax returns.

Register your business name with the government of your state if necessary. It is necessary to file a DBA (Doing Business As) form each time you operate a business under a name apart from your own. If you are conducting business under your own name as an independent contractor, you are exempt from needing one. If your business uses a name other than your own, you need to register it as a DBA.

• The place where you often register a DBA name is with your state's or county clerk's office. Because the process of registering varies from state to state, it is advised to conduct some web research before learning the precise requirements in your state. Usually, the registration process is completed in a short amount of time. Keep in mind that a DBA name is still required even if you are founding a corporation.

Since your business name is going to default to your name if you don't have a DBA, it is frequently useful for sole proprietorships.

Find out if your business requires a tax identification number. A corporation required to file tax returns as well as a partnership that does not file tax returns but is required to provide business information to the IRS annually will require one. If either of the following is in effect, you will need a separate tax ID number even though the IRS typically does not require one for a sole proprietorship since you are able to utilize your Social Security number instead:

• You employ people. You will want a tax ID in order to pay the payroll taxes that your company will be responsible for paying in half.

• You file tax returns pertaining to the employees of your business, excise, and the sale of alcohol, tobacco, and firearms.

Income that is not paid to non-resident aliens as wages is taxed.

• You hold a position in a non-profit, farmer cooperative, trustee, estate administrator, conduit for real estate mortgage investments, or plan administrator.

Make sure you have the necessary licenses and permits before starting your firm. Checking again to see whether you need any specific licenses or permits is a good idea. If you don't have the correct documentation, you could face fines or other consequences. For instance, if you offer to account for financial services, the majority of jurisdictions want a license.

• A permission or license from your county or city may also be required, therefore verify with your local government to be sure. Contacting your city, outlining your operation, and inquiring about any requirements is the simplest way to find out whether your particular firm needs any special licenses. For instance, many localities require "House Occupation Permits," which allow you to operate a business from your house.

You should register your trademarks and other proprietary information. Even though you will still need to cover necessary expenses, your ideas can help you end up making more money. In addition, they might provide you an edge over competitors, so be careful to register or patent them to guarantee your protection. Working with a lawyer is the greatest approach to protecting your intellectual property.

HOW TO SET UP YOUR WEBSITE

Make a decision regarding whether you want to create the site yourself or hire a designer. The cost of hiring a professional to create a well-designed website may be high. Consider your budget as well as the features you want from your website. Following that, you have the option of using a template or working with a designer. If you have web development experience, you could decide to build the site from scratch.

• Your website is built by web designers, who also choose your domain name and web host. The more money you invest, the more influence you'll have over creating a unique website.

• The cost of site design varies depending on whether you select a lone developer, an international web company, or a recognized US agency.

Why? The cost of e-commerce websites is frequently higher. To circumvent this, you can use your website for marketing purposes while connecting to a platform like Amazon or Etsy to complete the transaction.

Pick a web host if you're building your own website. A web host provides you with the space and support you need to manage your website. They are the actual owners of the servers that are used to host your website. Before selecting a web host, do your research on a few of them. Additionally, read customer reviews to get a feel of how satisfied clients are with various hosting services.

• Go with a company that offers first-rate technical help. In the event that your website is unavailable, this suggests that you should be able to contact someone for support. Your business is dependent on being accessible online, therefore any errors must be corrected immediately.

• Pick a website that backs up your website and automatically updates technical patches.

Register your domain name, either on your own or through your web host. Your internet business's domain name is its web address. Domain name registration requires contacting the Internet Corporation for Assigned Names and Numbers

(ICANN). To register your name for a year, you have to pay a registration fee of between $10 and $35. It needs to be renewed annually for the same cost. Though most web servers will take care of registering your domain for you, you could possibly able to avoid this step.

• Inquire as to whether your website host can register your domain on your behalf. Your user agreement's terms will provide more details.

Decide how you'll build your website if you're doing it yourself. The method you choose for creating a website will rely on your web design expertise, time constraints, and desired level of quality. Here are some alternatives:

• Utilize a template. Sites like WordPress, Square Space, and Wix all offer templates that can help you build a site that looks professional. While some templates are cost-free, others might have an additional fee.

Services like Moonfruit, Weebly, Qapacity, Jimdo, and Yola offer free business website construction; all you need to do is select a format and contribute content. Many are both free and offer reasonably priced upgrades for premium features.

• Request help from your state's or your Local business office. You can get free assistance in several states with building a company website. Look here for a list of state business offices.

Organize your website and add content. No matter if you build the site yourself or hire a designer, you will still need to generate the content that makes it up. Your content will likely include the following: • Descriptions and photos of products and services

• A brand's tagline or slogan

• A blog

• A professional or personal biography

• Client reviews

To improve the ranking of your website in search results, use search engine optimization (SEO). With the help of SEO, your website will appear at the top of search results. If you wish to, you can either do it yourself or engage a company to do it for you:

• Use keyword-rich material on the webpage. Utilize the Google Keyword Tool to find keywords that are similar to the words or expressions that clients would use to search for your products. Include these words and phrases across your website, including the homepage.

• Provide links to websites that you think your clients would find interesting. Links pointing to and from your website have an impact on its position in search results as well.

• Update your website frequently. As a result, your website will rise in the search results. Consider posting twice a week, and include keywords wherever you can. If you are not able to write substantially, often add photographs.

• Analyze the performance of your website's SEO using tools like Google Analytics.

You can either use e-commerce software or entrust transaction processing to a third party. Setting up a website hosted by a third party, such as Etsy, Shopify, or Amazon, might be easier. These websites might also provide superior technical support. As an alternative, you can incorporate an e-commerce platform directly into your website using tools like Squarespace, Magento, Bigcommerce, Woocommerce, or Webs. These services require a lot more time and technical expertise to utilize, despite being more resilient and customizable. If you're just starting an online business, a hosted solution is your best option. These services are easier to use and manage and work well for little purchases.

Make sure your website is user-friendly and professional. When building your website, keep in mind that its main purpose should be to market your good or service and facilitate sales. It must be as clear-cut and uncomplicated as possible. Best practices for creating a reliable website include the following:

• The website loads quickly, is usable on all devices and browsers and shows itself nicely.

• Using the website to make purchases and find the necessary information is simple.

• The website provides contact information, including your phone number;

• The website features nice photographs if you are offering physically tangible products that may be photographed.

MARKETING YOUR BUSINESS

Look into pay-per-click advertising. Buying traffic is the quickest way to generate visits to your website, and vendors allow you to utilize keyword searches to target certain regions. Ensure that you are concentrating on the right audience. You may lose money if numerous users browse your website but don't make a purchase if you pay for clicks. There are two notable advertisers:

• Google Ads: Your advertisements appear in the sidebar when users enter certain search terms that you specify.

• On social media (Facebook, Instagram, etc.), you may specify where your advertisement will appear as well as the audience's age, gender, and interests. The more specialized your audience is, the better your chances of success.

Build relationships and affiliate websites. Find trustworthy websites in your business and ask for permission to place ads there as a deal for them placing ads on their website. Sales are frequently made as a result of affiliate sites' high-quality traffic.

• For instance, if you own a business that teaches English to non-native speakers, you might want to get in touch with a trustworthy website that caters to recent immigrants. While they might gain access to your clientele by posting an ad on your website, doing so could boost traffic to yours.

Establish a social media presence. One in every seven minutes of American time is spent on social media, which presents a significant marketing potential. Create a presence where your clients are most likely to be first: on that platform.

• Establish a Facebook page. It should still exist even if it is not the business's main social media platform.

• Log on to Twitter.

• Use Instagram to interact with customers and educate them about your products or services.

• Upload movies to YouTube; post photographs of your products or images related to the services you provide. A helpful option for producing content that will simultaneously promote your company and educate visitors is YouTube. For instance, use YouTube to provide free investment content that relates to your products or services if your company offers a group-based website where consumers can get investment advice.

A word of advice: Be active on social media and post often, preferably several times per week and at least once daily. Images are a quick and easy way to do this. Inform your audience about sales, new arrivals, and other business-related news.

Online newsletter creation. Publication of a monthly or weekly newsletter is one of the best ways to take advantage of your email list. Make sure you provide worthwhile content that people want to engage with rather than intrusive sales pitches. If you're a graphic designer, for instance, give readers helpful information on how branding and graphic design techniques might be applied to entice new customers.

Consider creating a blog in addition to or as a substitute for an e-newsletter. A blog is a terrific way to expand your online clientele because every article you make has the potential to raise your ranking on search engines. As was previously stated, try to make your content useful rather than just a clear sales pitch. A recently released computer might be reviewed if you offer computer instruction, or if you're an accountant, you might discuss some new guidelines that have an influence on this year's taxes.

• Consider using a guest post. By contributing quality content to related blogs, you may show off your expertise and draw users to your website.

Make use of press releases. High-quality press releases are indexable by major search engines and many websites, and publishing one typically costs hundreds of dollars. Several wire services are available, like PR Newswire and PR Web.

Promote offline visits to your website. Mention your website to customers and friends, and be sure to publish the address of your website on all of your stationery, business cards, and brochures.

• Remember that the fact that your company is online does not imply you can't benefit greatly from traditional advertising techniques. This is especially true if your online or home-based business caters to or depends on local clients. For instance, contacts with surrounding businesses and organizations as well as web traffic can be quite beneficial for a graphic design firm.

• If your business fits this description, you may be interested in running advertisements on the radio or in the newspaper as well as taking part in regional networking events for your sector.

Observe client testimonials on sites like Yelp and Kudzu. Gaining positive online reviews is a great way to expand your business, and the most effective way to achieve it is by providing top-notch goods and friendly, courteous service. You should also be on the lookout for negative reviews so you can present your side of the story.

Beginning an Internet business is a little different than beginning a traditional business. Here are some essential steps you should take to start and develop your online business.

CHOOSE YOUR BUSINESS CONCEPT AND MARKET NICHE

Your business niche is the focus of your product or service's target market. Customers appreciate brands and businesses that cater to their unique needs, so choosing a niche is essential. Customers in general are considerably more inclined to purchase goods or services from a business that provides customized experiences.

Before choosing a niche and a company idea, ascertain the qualities of your target market, such as age range and hobbies. Next, utilizing the information you have learned, ascertain their major requirement. If your product doesn't meet a specific need, your firm won't succeed.

Conduct market analysis.

Conduct market research to decide what products or services to sell, whom to target, and where to look for the hardest competition. Whether your product is a physical object or a digital download, choosing the best placement depends on your understanding of your target market and the competition.

Utilize your knowledge to create a strong selling proposition. What sets your business apart from others, then? Why should someone buy from you?

Become familiar with the rules governing Internet commerce.

Even though Internet businesses might not require as many licenses and permissions as traditional businesses do, there are still legal requirements that you must abide by. Check carefully to see what kind of business license, if any at all, is necessary before you start operations.

Which legal arrangement is ideal for your company?

Do you require any permits or licenses?

Are there any inspections that you need to pass?

Are permits for sales tax required?

Exist any specific regulations that just relate to online businesses?

What laws govern hiring both employees and independent contractors?

Create a website.

After conducting your study, attending to the legalities, and focusing on your products or services, it is now time to develop your website. To be able to sell products online, your website needs to be built on a trustworthy eCommerce platform.

Set up shop.

As soon as your website is complete, you may begin adding products to your store. When adding your products, pay great attention to the images and descriptions of the products. Your viewers will find it simpler to explore your website if the image is clear and the explanation is comprehensive but concise.

It's critical to make sure that you provide your customers with a seamless shipping or delivery experience after you've finished setting up your store.

Make sure everything is working properly before pushing the "live" button on your website. Make sure that every link is clickable and that every page functions properly across all devices and browsers. Once you've checked that, you are ready to go live.

GROW YOUR BUSINESS

It's time to spread the word about your wonderful product now that you've created it. Or to put it another way, you need to reach more people. There are several ways to interact with your target market, such as: Using sponsored posts and hashtags on social media to reach a larger audience.

Using influencer marketing, send samples to "celebrities" in your niche.

Use Facebook groups to communicate with your target market.

Make your products accessible to internet consumers by using Google advertising.

Write blog entries as part of content marketing to boost organic site traffic.

Encourage customers to spread the news about your business.

Make a YouTube channel to advertise your products.

Chapter Seven

AVOIDING COMMON MISTAKES WHEN STARTING A BUSINESS

• Creating and implementing thorough plans for your business keeps your start-up on the path to success.

• By safely handling the finances of your business, you can avoid frequent financial risks;

• By being aware of the requirements that beginning a new business entails, you can better prepare for upcoming commitments.

Even though establishing a business is challenging, there are a lot of things you can do to ensure it is successful and lasts the first year.

When starting your business, stay away from these blunders.

A large number of new enterprises fail during the first two years, and more than fifty-five percent of businesses collapse within the first five years of operation. How then can you successfully launch and run your startup?

In this chapter, we'll look at the mistakes that startups most frequently make so that you can avoid them when starting your own business.

The fear of failing

Your worst error is to be paralyzed by fear of failure. Since failure is the key to success, facing your fear now will help your business much in the future. The ability to overcome obstacles and grow from mistakes is the key to extraordinary success.

Not preparing a business plan

Too many businesses start out without even a basic plan, and if you don't plan, you're truly planning to fail. For a new firm, even a one-page business plan is necessary. It must specify its operating expenses, expected sales, target market, and justification for product purchases.

Ineffective planning

Planning is essential. Being the head of the ring of a circus is analogous to small company management. Numerous things frequently occur simultaneously. I have a list of daily responsibilities that I rank in order of importance. Although it looks simple, it actually works and greatly boosts my productivity.

Not being specific enough about your target market and demographic

A common beginner mistake is not taking the time to fully understand the market or customers you are building a business for. If you don't regularly collect feedback from present or potential consumers, it's impossible to know if you're on the correct track. For technical founders, speaking with customers can appear easier than getting feedback from them. It's crucial to realize that creating excellent products does not always translate into a prosperous business. Many companies focus on a market that is too tiny to sustain a big corporation.

Not requesting the correct legal form

The biggest mistakes brand-new companies make are not registering, picking the wrong company entity, and failing to protect their intellectual property. These three factors must be taken into account in order to start a business properly since, if they are not, correcting the problems will be time- and money-consuming.

Doing everything on your own

The majority of the time, business owners make the error of believing they are self-sufficient and attempting to work alone without assistance from a professional. Don't launch a business by yourself, please. Consult reputable, knowledgeable experts about the concepts, tactics, difficulties, and growth of your business. A great deal of advice can serve as a source of power and understanding. In order to receive continual feedback and commit fewer mistakes, you should invite four people to join your company as advisers.

Interacting with the wrong investors

When starting a firm, entrepreneurs must understand that their shareholders are more than just financial backers. A company's original investors determine whether it succeeds or fails. These individuals have confidence in the company's potential despite not having seen a proof of concept. After collecting their initial seed funding, businesses will engage with investors who take the development and continued existence of the business into account.

Avoiding contracts

One of the most common errors an entrepreneur or business owner can make when starting a company is failing to execute contracts. No matter how good a relationship may be, if agreements and terms are not in place, it could terminate unexpectedly.

Initial hiring

The worst mistake a business can make is hiring workers too early. It is also not advisable to hire full-time workers when part-time workers could make more financial sense or hiring staffs when subcontractors would have performed the same job. Running a small business is surprisingly easy with the aid of contractors, subcontractors, and other specialists.

Minimizing the requirement for financing

Most business owners believe they can accomplish more with less. They fail to take into consideration any roadblocks, problems, or holdups along the way in an effort to lessen equity dilution. Startup leaders routinely forecast optimistic results, but this hardly ever happens. This type of thinking could be linked to leaders' self-indulgence and optimism. But when it comes to raising money, optimism has its limits because it frequently calls for returning to the well for a less-than-ideal rise.

Wasting money

Unscrupulous cash flow management and poor money management are death sentences for companies with limited access to finance. Without a clear plan in place to manage the end of the funnel, I made the error of spending money to hire too many employees rather than choosing the right experts to staff the peak of the funnel, and I also recruited too many individuals. Striking to meet everyone's demands rather than concentrating on a niche market is a surefire way to waste the time and money that is the lifeblood of every startup.

Paying yourself too little or too much

Paying yourself too little or too much is a mistake. A new employee's salary is typically easier to ascertain than that of the owner or a partner. Consider setting aside a portion of your income for yourself. Whatever you choose, make it the norm and the foundation of a sound management expectation to calculate your income and the salaries of your partners.

Wrong pricing

Don't set pricing that is either too expensive or too low if you intend to grow your market share. If you are skilled at it, price it! A lot of entrepreneurs start out with the greatest of intentions, giving away things or doing things for free to support a good cause, their neighborhood, or get attention. Use considerable caution with this since you don't want to be seen as a source of freebies. Make a start by ringing the till.

Taking off earlier than necessary

One of the most common mistakes made by business owners is starting before they are ready. The saying "Done is better than perfect" is sound advice, but it calls for the "done" to be able to serve more customers. Make sure your systems and processes, including contracts, communications, payment conditions, and procedures, are in place once you have gone public and are getting clients so that you can continue to carry out your marketing strategy. You need to make sure your back-end processes are perfect before taking on clients because else, these shortcomings will become obvious and give the impression that you lack professionalism.

An excessive rate of expansion

It's easy to believe that development continues once you begin to succeed, and that the easiest way to take advantage of this is to just replicate your winning formula. However, if you expand your business too quickly, it could have disastrous effects. Your period of expansion can turn out to be fleeting, leaving you with a huge number of new employees but no work and no money to pay for them. It's imperative to grow gradually as a result, and you should never react to an unanticipated surge of success.

Not following the right bookkeeping process

Many startup owners launch their businesses without an accounting system in place. Making educated business decisions, spotting opportunities early, and resolving problems before they spiral out of hand are all made possible by good bookkeeping procedures. It is simpler to keep track of your company's financial health if you are familiar with your finances. Effective bookkeeping practices also ensure that you stay on top of responsibilities like insurance and tax obligations, which can pose issues for otherwise excellent businesses.

Not creating a marketing strategy

You must have a strategy for how you are going to acquire your first user, first 10 users, first 100 customers, etc. once the problem, market, and idea for the business have been effectively proven. Determining how to get users, turn those users into paying customers, and keep them happy enough to recommend your product to others all require a comprehensive marketing strategy.

Using the wrong individuals

You'll need to hire people with certain skill sets and qualifications for each of the numerous positions. Make sure you have dependable generalists who can handle everything when you first start. When your company begins to grow, take into account appointing employees with particular abilities to the jobs that require them. Don't hire someone with particular expertise when a person with general expertise would be more suitable, and don't hire a generalist when a specialist would be better suited.

Making extravagant or unfulfilled promises

Don't overwork yourself in an effort to make money. Telling a prospective client that you can do their job next month, for example, is considered preferable to taking on too much. In addition to keeping you from falling short of your objectives due to an increased workload, doing this will give the appearance that you are in great demand. That's always advantageous.

Lowering the bar for business expectations

The largest mistake new businesses make is underestimating the needs of the firm. Documentaries and blogs about startups are encouraging people more since they focus on the business' successes rather than the challenges of starting one in the first place. As a result, people incorrectly think that starting a business is easy and fun when, in reality, the reverse is true. Startups are where you spend most of your money and time. It even has the power to end relationships.

Starting your company off right

A great organization must be built as a team, therefore surround yourself with mentors and subject-matter specialists you can trust. Instead of being afraid of failing, learn from your failures and make any required improvements to your company's strategy. Test new ideas and solicit feedback to enhance your product and better satisfy customer needs.

There are a few startup mistakes you'll want to avoid when building your business, but mistakes will unavoidably occur occasionally. While going through the procedure, be kind to yourself. One of the best things you can do is to take what would initially seem to be bad news, learn from it, and use it to your benefit. With such a perspective, business success might be right around the corner.

51657163R00075